TO THE TEACHER

This unit contains four transparencies and four double–sided reproducible pages for student and teacher use. Each double–sided reproducible includes a duplicate of the transparency illustration on one side, allowing students to have a copy to color, label, and refer to as needed. Students may keep these copies in individual portfolios. The reverse side of each reproducible includes related classroom activities to pursue, and can be copied for student use where indicated by an * in the text below.

Key concepts emphasized in **Apples** include habitat, community, growth, change, structure, function, relationships, interdependency, and variety.

Key skills include investigating, observing, communicating, identifying, describing, classifying, and recording.

Key curriculum areas include science, language arts, mathematics, and social studies.

Key vocabulary words are indicated in bold type within the *Background Material;* many also appear as labels on the transparencies.

NOTE: Classroom emphasis on specific concepts, skills, curricular areas, or vocabulary will vary depending on grade level, interest, and developmental readiness of students.

APPLES: Background Material

History, Legend, & Location of Apple Trees
TRANSPARENCY #1

Apples were introduced in America by European settlers who brought apple seeds with them when they journeyed to the New World. The first apple trees were planted in Massachusetts within a few years of the Pilgrims' arrival. Apple trees could withstand the cold New England winters, and the climate provided the warmth and sunshine necessary for producing blossoms and fruit during spring and summer months. In the fall, enough apples could be harvested to last throughout the winter.

From New England, apples spread to other parts of America as early pioneers left the eastern seaboard to explore westward just before the turn of the 18th century. One of those early pioneers was John Chapman, more commonly known as **Johnny Appleseed**. Legend has it that he walked the westward trails in his bare feet, with only a potato sack for a shirt and a cooking pot for a hat. In winter, he bound his feet in rags. In his knapsack, he carried apple seeds, and planted them at each settlement along his journey west. The majority of Johnny Appleseed's trees were planted in the Ohio Valley, in the states known today as Ohio, Indiana, and Illinois. The legend and legacy surrounding Johnny Appleseed are still with us today. *Duplicate reproducible page 2 for students as you prepare apples in different ways as a classroom activity. This activity may also be shared at home with parents.*

Structure, Function, & Importance of Apple Trees
TRANSPARENCY #2

The apple **tree** is important to people, who use its fruit for eating, cooking, and making cider. But it is also important to other animals. Birds and squirrels might build nests in its **branches**. Sometimes a hollow **trunk** of an apple tree becomes a home for animals such as raccoons. Other animals such as beetles, ants, or other insects live on or beneath the **bark** of the apple tree. Woodpeckers might peck into the bark, searching for ants or other insects to eat. Honeybees or butterflies will drink nectar from the **apple blossom**, pollinating the **flowers** with pollen dust as they fly from one flower to another (*see also Transparency #3 below*). Other animals, like ravens, mice, and deer, eat apples as part of their diet. All of the creatures who use the apple tree for food or shelter are part of a **community** of living things which the tree supports. *Duplicate reproducible page 4 for students to complete.*

Through the **seasons** of the year, the apple tree **changes**. In **spring**, its branches produce **leaves** and **blossoms** which burst open from **buds**. The flowers have a sweet smell, and the air around the tree is filled with the sound of buzzing bees. In **summer**, the **crown** of the tree is covered with deep green leaves, and the apple **fruit** appears. In **autumn (fall)**, the fruit is ripe and ready to **harvest**. The leaves turn yellow and eventually fall to the ground, along with any remaining fruit, leaving the branches bare. In **winter**, the tree undergoes a resting period before "waking" to bloom again in the spring. Its buds are covered with a fuzzy hair that protects them from the cold. (See also *Oaks Thematic Unit* listed in the bibliography.)

Blossoms, Pollination, & Growth of Apples
TRANSPARENCY #3

Apples are the **fruit** of the apple tree. They are produced when the apple blossom has been **pollinated** by a **honeybee** or other insect during the warm spring season. Honeybees fly only when the temperature is above 65°F (18°C). An apple blossom on one tree must be cross–pollinated by pollen from the blossom of a different apple tree. Often, apple growers will keep beehives close to the apple orchards to ensure a large enough supply of bees for cross–pollination. (See also *Honeybees Thematic Unit* listed in the bibliography.)

Apple blossoms are either white or pink **flowers**. Each flower has five **petals**. The center of each flower contains the **pistil** and the **stamens** which are, respectively, the female and male parts of the flower. Pollen–covered **anthers** are located at the top of each stamen. Pollination takes place when **pollen** from an anther is transferred by honeybees to the sticky top of the pistil, called the **stigma**. The transfer occurs when pollen sticks to tiny hairs on the body of the honeybee. Pollen then travels in tubes from the stigma, down through the **style**, and then to the **ovary** at the lower end of the pistil. As the flower ripens, its petals fade, and the ovary begins to swell. The ovary contains **ovules** which, when fertilized by pollen, become apple **seeds**. The swollen ovary continues to grow, becoming the fleshy apple that contains the seeds. *Duplicate reproducible page 6 for students to complete.*

Every apple contains an arrangement of **seeds** inside. The seeds are surrounded by the **flesh** of the apple, which is in turn surrounded by the **skin**. The seeds are housed within **five chambers** in the **core** of the apple. Each seed can produce another apple tree. But the seeds must first undergo a dormant period in a cold, moist environment, where they can ripen before planting. (See also *Plants Thematic Unit* listed in the bibliography.) *Students can try sprouting apple seeds, following the instructions outlined on reproducible page 6.*

There are several thousand varieties of apples grown throughout the world, but only a few kinds are usually available at local grocery or produce markets. Bring several into the classroom for students to cut open and taste. *Duplicate the chart on reproducible page 8 so students can record their observations.*

Some of the more common varieties:

Winesap	Bright red, juicy, hard, crisp, tart. Small white dots on skin. Okay for raw eating or for cooking.
Baldwin	Large, red, hard, juicy, tart. Good for baking whole or in making applesauce.
McIntosh	Dark red with stripes, juicy, somewhat tart. Good for raw eating or using in cold salad.
Red Delicious	Deep red, firm, sweet. Five bumps or knobs on the blossom end. Good for raw eating or using in cold salads.
Rome Beauty	Largest apple sold; thick red skin. Good for baked apples. Poor for raw eating.
Granny Smith	Yellowish green. Tart, juicy. Excellent for raw eating.
Golden Delicious	Yellow, sweet, crisp. Good for raw eating, for making applesauce, pies, baking whole, or using in cold salads.
Jonathon	Bright red, often with yellow cavity at stem end. Crisp, tender, juicy, sweet, tart. Excellent for both raw eating and cooking.

ADDITIONAL ACTIVITIES

1. Geography: Draw a large outline map of the United States. Pin it to a bulletin board. Use an encyclopedia to find out which states are the largest growers of apple trees. Have students cut out small "tree shapes" and pin them to these areas of the map. Draw in the state boundary lines. Place labels with state names on those states growing large numbers of apple trees.

2. Social Studies/Drama: Johnny Appleseed dispersed many apple seeds. Find out more about his life and activities. Have the students create a classroom play about him.

3. Social Studies: Find out how apples are transferred from tree to market.

4. Language Arts/Social Studies: Find out about other legends, lore, or superstitions associated with apples. For example: sayings such as, "As American as apple pie," or "An apple for the teacher," or "The Big Apple," in reference to New York City; stories about William Tell, Sir Isaac Newton, or others.

5. Language Arts: Make a list with students of all the words they can think of that describe apples. Encourage them to think about size, shape, color, smell, texture, taste. Examples might be: red, green, crunchy, round, sweet, sour, juicy, hard, shiny, fresh, rotten, delicious, etc.

6. Math: 1) Emphasize measurement in following the recipes included in this unit, reproducible page 2.
2) Compare sizes or weights of apples used in recipes.
3) Emphasize the terms "whole, half, quarter" as you cut apples for each recipe.

7. Science: Find out about other fruits that grow on trees. Cut them open to investigate the insides and to taste. In what ways are they the same as, or different from, the apple? Examples are: pear, peach, cherry, plum, apricot, grapefruit, orange, avocado. Use copies of the chart on reproducible page 8 in this unit for recording student observations.

8. Science: Find out how honeybees live, locate flowers, and make honey. Taste apple blossom honey. Invite a local apple orchard grower or beekeeper to speak to your class about how apples grow, and about the important relationship between bees and apple blossoms.

9. Science/Social Studies: Find out how apple cider is made. Taste apple cider and apple juice. How are they alike? Different?

10. Science/Health: Does "An apple a day keep the doctor away"? Find out why apples are a healthy food to eat.

11. More foods from apples: Make apple butter, apple pie, candied apples.

BIBLIOGRAPHY

Aliki. *The Story of Johnny Appleseed*. New Jersey: Prentice-Hall, 1963.

Follman, Ilene L. *Honeybees Thematic Unit*. St. Louis: Milliken Publishing Co., 1993.

——. *Oaks Thematic Unit*. St. Louis: Milliken Publishing Co., 1995.

Johnson, Sylvia A. *Apple Trees*. Minneapolis: Lerner Publications Co., 1983.

Maestro, Betsy. *How Do Apples Grow?* New York: Harper Collins Children's Books, 1992.

Martin, Alice A. *All About Apples*. Boston: Houghton Mifflin Co., 1976.

Micucci, Charles. *The Life and Times of the Apple*. New York: Orchard Books, 1992.

Nottridge, Rhoda. *Apples*. Minneapolis: Carolrhoda Books, Inc., 1991.

Ortleb, Edward P. *Plants Thematic Unit*. St. Louis: Milliken Publishing Co., 1995.

Parnall, Peter. *Apple Tree*. New York: Macmillan Publishing Co., 1987.

Patent, Dorothy Hinshaw. *An Apple a Day: From Orchard to You*. New York: Cobblehill Books/Dutton, 1990.

Schnieper, Claudia. *An Apple Tree Through the Year*. Minneapolis: Carolrhoda Books, Inc., 1987.

Selsam, Millicent E. *The Apple and Other Fruits*. New York: William Morrow & Co., 1973.

ANSWERS

Page 4: community **Page 5:** ovary

APPLES

History, legend, and location of apple trees

Below is a drawing of Johnny Appleseed and a map of the United States. Color the state that you live in. Draw apple trees on the map to show the places where Johnny Appleseed planted seeds as he traveled westward.

Name

APPLES

In the classroom: Recipes to try

Try some of these recipes with your students. As they prepare the apples in different ways, emphasize how the different processes *(cooking, drying, chopping)* change the apples.

Applesauce

1/2 red apple per child   granulated sugar
1/2 cup water   ground cinnamon

1) Wash apples. Cut them into quarters and cut each quarter in half. Remove the core, seeds, and stems. DO NOT PEEL.
2) Place all apple pieces in a large cooking pot. Add the water. Bring apples to a boil on a stove or hot plate; reduce heat and cook gently until soft.
3) Use a long–handled wooden spoon to mash and stir the apple mixture.
4) Use a slotted spoon to transfer sauce to a serving bowl. Let cool. Give each student a small portion to taste. Students may add a small amount of sugar or cinnamon if desired.

Dried Apple Rings

several whole apples, enough for 1/2 apple per student *(tart varieties are best)*

1) Use a coring knife to core each apple.
2) Peel each apple.
3) Slice each cored, peeled apple into rings, approximately 1/4" (6mm) thick.
4) Thread the apple rings onto a length of string or twine. Be certain each ring does not touch the one next to it. Hang the apple rings indoors by fastening the ends of the twine to the inside of a window frame or other convenient location. It will take approximately two weeks for the apple rings to dry. *(Outdoor drying in a dry climate may be quicker, but insects may feast on the rings in the process unless the rings are covered with a fine netting or cheese-cloth.)* Once the rings are dry, distribute them to the students for a tasty treat.

Apple, Carrot, and Raisin Salad

1/2 apple per student   1 carrot per student
raisins   mayonnaise

1) Remove core and seeds from apples. DO NOT PEEL. Cut apples into small pieces.
2) Peel carrots; shred using a grater.
3) Combine cut apples and shredded carrots in a large bowl.
4) Add raisins.
5) Add just enough mayonnaise to moisten the mixture of apples, carrots, and raisins; serve.

Name

APPLES

An apple tree

Below is an apple tree in fall, full of ripe apples. Write the names of the apple tree parts on the lines provided. Use the space below the picture to draw some animals that might live in or by the tree.

Name

APPLES

The life of an apple tree

Below are some animals that are partners with the apple tree. Some of the animals like to eat apples. These animals help the apple tree to spread its seeds Some like to drink sweet juice from flowers on the tree. These animals help the tree to make more seeds. Other animals make their homes in apple trees.

Which animals can you name? Write each name on the line beneath the animal. Draw lines to connect each animal with the part of the tree it might like best.

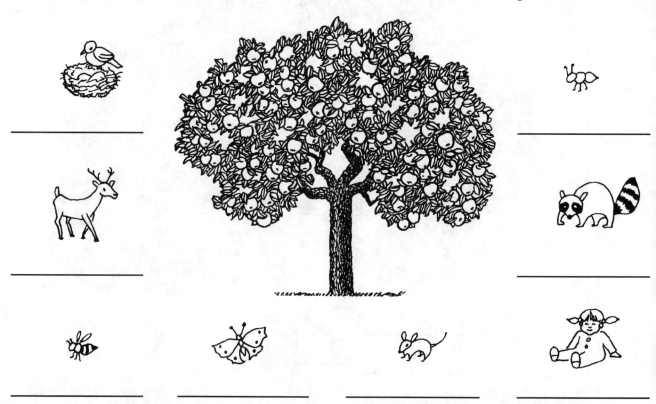

Use the picture code to help you find the missing word in the sentence below.

c	i	h	m	n	o	u	t	y

Many animals live in the apple tree. This makes the tree a

___ ___ ___ ___ ___ ___ ___ ___ ___ of living things.

APPLES

Apple flowers

Color the pictures on this page.

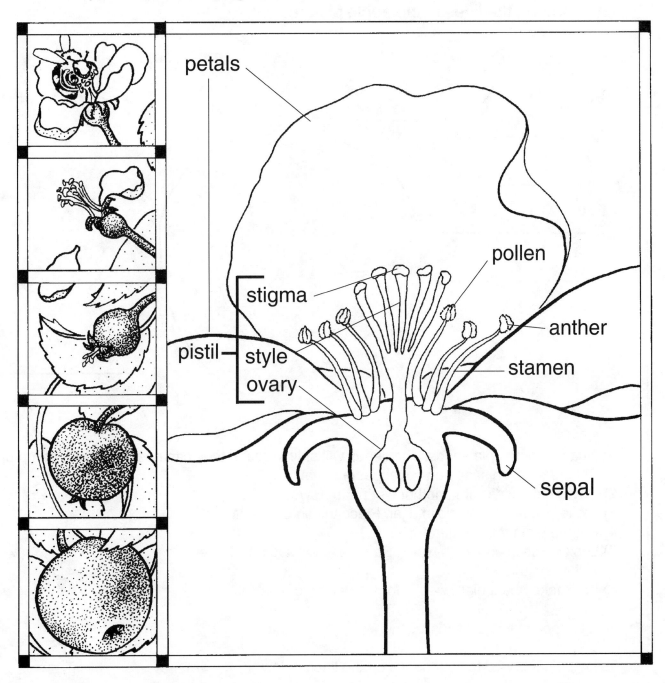

Which part of the flower becomes the apple fruit?

___ ___ ___ ___ ___

APPLES

Inside an apple

Find the names of the apple parts in the list of words below. Write the names of each part on the lines in the apple picture.

skin   flesh   seeds   stem   core

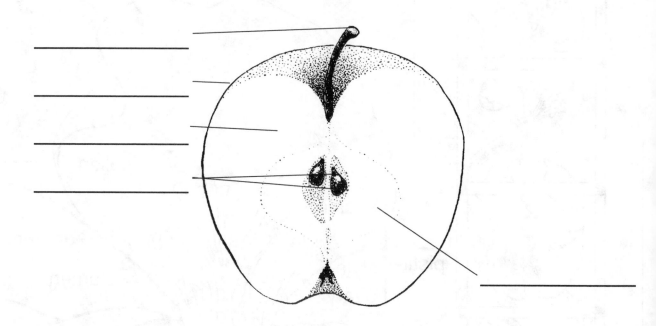

You can sprout apple seeds. The seeds will only sprout if they can ripen in a cold, damp place.
1) Put some apple seeds on a wet paper towel.
2) Cover the seeds with another wet paper towel.
3) Place seeds and towels in a jar. Place the lid on the jar.
4) Put the jar in the refrigerator.
5) Look at the seeds each week. Be sure to always return them
   to the refrigerator.
6) It will take about eight weeks for the seeds to change.

What happens to the seeds?

Tell what happened to your seeds on the lines below.

_____

_____

_____

Name

APPLES

Inside an apple

Color the whole apples below. Draw a circle around the half apples.
Draw a square around the quarter apples.

Name

APPLES

Finding things out about apples

Use this chart to record your observations about apples. You can compare and contrast the color, size, taste, smell, crispness, juiciness, number of seeds, or other characteristics of a variety of apples that you have cut open and tasted.

Name _____

Hard or Soft

Name of Apple	Skin	Taste	Juicy Yes	No	Crunchy Yes	No	Number of Seeds	Other Observations

NOTES

NOTES